MISCHIEF

Peter Bennet lived for over thirty years near the Wanney Crags in Northumberland, in a remote cottage associated with the ballad-writer James Armstrong, author of 'Wild Hills o' Wannys'. He now lives in Whitley Bay.

His Bloodaxe retrospective, *Border* (2013), includes work from books including *Goblin Lawn* (2005), a Poetry Book Society Recommendation, *The Glass Swarm* (2008), a Poetry Book Society Choice which was shortlisted for the T.S. Eliot Prize, and *The Game of Bear* (2011), all published by Flambard Press, and features his four major sequences, *The Long Pack*, *Jigger Nods*, *Folly Wood* and *Bobby Bendick's Ride*, as well as a selection of new poems. His latest collection, *Mischief*, was published by Bloodaxe in 2018. He has also published several pamphlets, including collaborations with the artist Birtley Aris.

PETER BENNET

Mischief

BLOODAXE BOOKS

ISBN: 978 1 78037 440 6

First published 2018 by
Bloodaxe Books Ltd,
Eastburn,
South Park,
Hexham,
Northumberland NE46 1BS.

www.bloodaxebooks.com
For further information about Bloodaxe titles
please visit our website and join our mailing list
or write to the above address for a catalogue

Supported using public funding by

**ARTS COUNCIL
ENGLAND**

Cover design: Neil Astley & Pamela Robertson-Pearce.

Printed in Great Britain by Bell & Bain Limited, Glasgow, Scotland, on
acid-free paper sourced from mills with FSC chain of custody certification.

For Sue

ACKNOWLEDGEMENTS

Acknowledgements are due to the editors of the following publications in which some of these poems first appeared: *The Compass, The High Window, Island* (Australia), *The North, Shadow Script: twelve poems for Lindisfarne and Bamburgh* (NCLA, 2013) and *The Times Literary Supplement.*

CONTENTS

9   The Place I Am

10   The Riddle

11   Miss Hood in the Nursing Home

12   Old Fashioned

13   Auberge

14   The Unsafe Landing

15   Tales of Tesco

16   Boustrophedon Lang Syne

18   The Comfort Service

19   The Leopard

20   The Laboratory

21   *La Morale de Joujou*

22   A Helpmeet for Protestant Mystics

23   The Muse and the Fridge

24   The Heiress

25   Like Me

26   Three of Us

27   Listening to Bees

28   The Old Stacks

29   The Better Place

30   After Dark at Lindisfarne Castle

31   Gantries

32   The Magic Castle

33   The Unicorn

34   Remission

35   LANDSCAPE WITH PSYCHE

42   The Turtle Holiday

43   Proxy

44   Next Time

45   The Winpole Boy

46   After Pevsner

47   The Nuisances

48   Pastoral

49   The Ornithologist

50   Resting Rats

51   Virgil

52   French Windows

53   The Philosopher

54   Barefooted

55   The Trouser Button

56   Sanquar

57   LADDEREDGE AND COTISLEA

67   The Gypsy Fiddle

68   The Columns

69   The Vapour Trail

70   An Exhibition Catalogue

71   Death and the Spinster

72   The Cormorant

73   Seasons

74   News of a Death

75   My Mother at Erbistock

76   A Piano in Hobart

79   NOTES

The Place I Am

I have become a master of the craft
of moulding, patiently and with precision,
lethargy into shapes of hours and days.
My cast of mind requires a library
of books I wrote myself, sufficient booze
and shabby furniture. Beyond
the balcony is marshy coast. My gaze
slides along pewter-coloured horizontals
that evening sunlight turns to bronze.
It is a habitat where rare plants learn
to live with salt, and birds nest on the ground.
It is the place I am. It should be empty
of any presence otherwise.
Rage and tales of unmapped quicksand
are not discouraging enough.
The landscape fades. I fade. I mourn its beauty
leached into sketch and photograph
or into notebooks that birdwatchers carry.
The sea is close. I fear death by erosion.
It has grown dark but now the sky is starry.
I'll jot down where I'd like my body found
but not by whom. I think that's better left.
And better left, I also think, is when.
The airport glows inland. A homing plane
blinks across the ankles of Orion.

The Riddle

The first anthropological axiom of the Evil One is not
All men are evil, but *All men are the same*.

W.H. AUDEN

Promise, Son, when you address appearances,
that you won't fall for similarity
and finish up like I am, unaware
of variation. Steer clear of revery
in case you subsequently fail to wake
to what things actually are or were.
Differentiation is essential work
requiring recognition accurate
as a marksman's rifle. Seek clarity.
If any object does not have a name
then name it. Learn by heart all essences.
Go nowhere on the train. Avoid the state
that I got into, me and my poor father,
not spotting on the platform among people
very much unlike each other
the beast that leapt – the stench of it – beside us –
straight through the carriage window glass remember –
its wet tongue pressed to the first syllable
of the riddle which makes everything the same.
That finished Dad. And as for me?
I dream all day of what I most resemble.

Miss Hood in the Nursing Home

There are at all times footsteps on the landing.
It's March. Last autumn's last leaves hop and hope
like ghosts of frogs to find their late
lives in the pools of air the bare trees hold
outside her window. She'll undress
and go to bed an hour to stretch
the day a little and then scold
her mind for wandering as it resolves
to call for Matron and confess
that she has fairytale for memory
and can't afford to stay at Grateloup.
She'll make for one more time the intimate
attempt to constitute the 'I'
without which we shall have no understanding.
Good. Good. Her eyelids have begun to twitch
in that exact way we term *gratum lupis*
which means of course agreeable to wolves.

Old Fashioned

She is the big star of the cinema
inside my head. She condescends
to bring to life the films I dream. She'll be
exactly as I want her. Let's say *bold*
and *smouldering*. Tonight she plays
a war-time Cockney with a grin –
the darling of the blitz among the bombsites
and unlit frog-and-toads. A waste
of talent but it bucks me up. It ends
where it begins in blurring blacks and whites
of sinking arctic convoys. I can't resist
the scene where she chats up this chap
a lot like you but with more taste:
First point, Big Boy, make sure the Bourbon's hold.
'Alf a lump of sugar. No hangostura.
Just the Bourbon. Fill up with a load o' hice
then float a slice o' horange on the top.
Don't squeeze it. Hadd a cherry for the colour.
Sultry stuff. She nearly melts the cocktail-glass
besides the screen and camera.
Why not cut yourself some action? Improvise.
Inveigle her onto the balcony
to watch the fountain – in the final clip
with Churchill on the brandy in the garden –
cast its plume. But don't imagine
even flattered by my indoor seachlights
that you'll get lucky as fresh bombs fly in.

Auberge

I hope you like your room. You overlook
the entrance to the crematorium.
Even if you oversleep you're sure to wake
in time to catch at least one funeral.
The lingering scent of wreaths in drizzle
will be consoling, like the glare and hum
in your ensuite at midnight and the thump
of water pressure maximum. The climate
is hopeful hereabouts. We cope with that
by clinging to despair. We're private people.
If you require assistance, pray. Don't come
to find us or your fellow guests. To peek
and pry is bad taste and a theft of knowledge.
We keep no record of the time or date.
When you decide to go please sign the book.
You'll find the tablets in your bedside fridge.

The Unsafe Landing

Late sunbeams are prodigious epicures
in the realms of mould and small collapses –
frequent in their favourite places –
and connoisseurs of arabesques
rats sketch in dust. Let's watch them blaze
through bleary glass and lap the floors
and walls then climb as sun goes down to graze
the ceiling of some unsafe landing. Risks
must be run for such apocalypses.
Their tongues explore the flavour of our faces.

Tales of Tesco

Five swift-limbed dogs were once laid down
beneath the tarmac by the car-park exit.

Their spirits leave the ground in joy
and all directions, rummaging.

We run behind them for our feet are glad.

There go three matrons and a shining child.

They know our troubles and will bless us.

The bearded god, attended by two pigeons,
who ducks his head in squeezing forth
from that small turquoise sports car is a man
who taught me nothing years ago
at school and is deceased. He lives again
because I wish to send him voyaging
among a hundred gilded boats
to find the happy otherworld
and sample islands for their types of beauty.

We shall go with him on his pilgrimage.

The ticket machine that totals up the hours
there in the noon light where the trolleys wait
beside the automatic doors
will cry out loudly at the touch
of any true king or a king's true son.

It whispers news of feasting and great profit.

The meaning of the litter bin
relates to that of wells or graves, therefore
approach with reverence. Drop something in.

Boustrophedon Lang Syne

Last evening Present was the guest of Past
colloquy their died December as and
begun uneasily began to deepen
.back turn would it paused it time every and
He struggled to think Is not Was
name her speak to care good took but
as if it held significance.
menagerie his paddocks long-lost In
ailed as Winter stalled. The moon forbore to rise.
Potentiality about asked She
of flowers' colours, for example, latent
.bud and seed the in fragrance like
He said that though his skull holds nothing new
.it in already course of are questions such
He then fell silent but a catch
.lick smoke a provoked throat chimney's the in
A log cracked and a quick flame spoke.
capers the about notes jotting he's Today
– prancing one way then the other –
Future with cut him make moments
in fading pictographs on papyrus,
.bits to them tearing then distractedly
The weather's mild. If he's correct
spotted last was seeking is she answer the
one February stretching into March
stones over foaming melt snow in deep knee
approached through brambles and on muddy grass
.odours wet good and ripple-sounds by guided
He clicks his jaw to smile and offers her
.picnic-basket cobwebbed a and thermos a
She must say Thankyou, go, and then return.
skeletons watch will they Hogmanay Next
of every year there ever was

toe to toe and rib tickling rib
galumph like super-sized albino spiders
visit and ossuary private his at
Potentiality, who lives nearby,
.plough to job her is it fields the among

The Comfort Service

Our broadcasts are addressed to those bereaved
who cannot acquiesce to separation.
We keep things cheerful and include
favourites of the deceased. There's Little Nell,
Tagore and Keats, that episode
with Greta Garbo and the lion.
The actors we employ do not intone
inside their bowler hats like once-revered
announcers on the wireless talking rain.
But should you wish you may select Received
Pronunciation. Or indeed Morse Code.
We simply bring to bear the miracle
of narrative. There's no wrong time or place
to switch on and tune in. Clear as a bell.
The topic for today? 'What I Most Feared
Before I Made a Friend of Fright.'
We do provide advice, now and again,
which might be, sometimes, for example:
'Dear listener, look past the much-loved face
to greater love, where death cannot profane
its memory, or hog the light.'

The Leopard

The district is *moins cher* but the address
is decent. She's in the parlour
in which she breakfasted. It has been tidied
for her to read or write or not.
This is the top floor. There is a cellar
far below with stone steps to a deeper one.
Her nearest window looks down at the courtyard
and a cane chair set out by the concierge
in case of sun. The other frames a view
of roofs of narrow houses and bare trees,
pigeons and sky. It's time to go.
Somewhere a long way off and tropical.
If only she can pull herself together
she need not ever call to mind again
that coffin or museum cabinet
she dreams of here or dust and scraps of cloth
which are the shreds of what she's wearing now.
C'est bon. She's picturing a crocodile
that's basking in digestive sloth
and shallow mud. She is the cheerful leopard
that bats its snout with a mischievous paw
then saunters into foliage
with a leopard's cough but with a woman's smile.

The Laboratory

I've waited here all night lit by the glum
red bulbs above the warning notices.
Pull up the blinds and throw light on the tools
that I thought up and helped you make
when you were still unsure about the rules
and over-sensitive and prone to worries.
I'm near you in the dust above the benches
and angular uncomfortable stools
but you don't see. You're half asleep
and at the window as some water bird
hops across grass and then takes wing
to launch itself upon the lake
and on the surface of your mind like beauty.
You rub your chin until your jaw unclenches
then press your forehead and begin to weep.
I know your conscience has been saying Wrong
and reason has said Stop but, trust me, duty
though painful does not make us ghouls.
Throw back the doors. The beneficiaries
of our research already come
limping down the un-signposted access road
or clinging to the sides of dark slow lorries.

La Morale de Joujou

Here's a jewellery box and here's the river
that's on the best page of her favourite book
and here's a child who wants to see
the soul of things. She will interrogate
whatever's nearby and inanimate
especially what she's told to leave alone
and love it half to death. Alas
things must repeat *her* stories not their own.
The box she wrenches open and upends
is delicately made but it's the picture
she chews and crumples that provides most fun.
And who knows how things happen. Look.
The river's twisting like a snake with songs
comprising hissing sounds and liquid kisses
and wraps itself around us as it sings.
It's time we both grew out of make-believe.
While I relax on warm dry grass
I think she'll push herself to deeper water
with one last infant kick and then swim under
to learn how life could start to be
among the quick imaginary fishes.

A Helpmeet for Protestant Mystics

She limps. She is inadequately shod
and not dressed for the weather of the mind.
She needs to feel her way with arms extended
to grope the insides of our skulls.
As soon as she is with or even near us
we start to see. Without her we are blind.

She quiets us to let us hear
applause again that led to curtain calls,
when we were young, for Agape and Eros
in theatres of bliss. She has amended
the chart of routes between our names for God.
She is the kinder sister of Dame Kind.

The Muse and the Fridge

Open your mind and see the light come on.
Feel the cool as you become the notion
of a thinking fridge that's chock-a-block
with insight that will be delicious
now that it's ripe. I like my scran.
There is no question of conflicting wills.
I am in charge. I have the run
of the kitchen in your head. I'll keep you stocked
with aperçus I wish to chill
then gobble up. Today I downright fancy
a certain very succulent perception
you've had since Spring inside your shivery brain.
When I have made a meal of it you'll see
that what you meant to say began
as dead stink of forgotten daffodils
in a neglected vase. Await digestion.
Keep humming. You have still to serve your purpose.
Please do not second-guess what I have done.

The Heiress

It's time to please myself. Perhaps to travel.
But now a gentleman with tear-stained cheeks
weeps between two packing cases
and though he can't make sense for sobbing speaks.
Perhaps he's found one of the anti-lamps
dear Father always promised to devise
to prove that customers will gladly pay
for obfuscation when the need arises.
He sprawls there like a murky glimpse
of heartbreak on the Morris rug.
Should I unbend and help him up?
Since he consists so fully of devotion
he might turn out to be a prudent move
if I proceed to let my life unravel
entirely into fashion and distraction.
I can afford to let him hope
a while at least. Why not call back my luggage.
Of course he is impossible to love.
But he loves me. He'll be the first of many.
I see that clearly as he dries his eyes
and blinks them in the light of Daddy's money.

Like Me

The afternoon has paused and hollyhocks
overlook me and the dolls I have set out
along with Teddy Bear beside the shoes
of the man who talks at us because he's old.
We sit cross-legged on the lawn and pay
attention like a family. He speaks
of circumstances where he did not flinch
when challenged by his fellow officers
to eat a wine glass. Anecdotes are dim
lanes coiling in a labyrinth
of escapades. They lead to bottlenecks
where he turns fretful and asks me the way.
It's off to bed for dolls and bear.
But I'm grown up. I check his every inch
of face for liver-spots and pass the time
by itemising wrinkles. Mould
is growing on the shoulder of his coat.
He has a runny nose. It's getting cold.
We stand. His rise is lizardly.
He knows he must know someone like me somewhere.
And I remember that I married him.

Three of Us

Breathing asks and answers its own question.
Shadows move on grass. A Roman altar
converted by some ancestor
into a sundial says late afternoon.
It usually does. It's getting warm.
I shan't bestir myself to walk across
and see if I can make out the inscription.
You're back now with a photograph
of that lost chum of ours, the scallywag
as good as bad luck when you need it most,
who'd always take a joke, and liked the charm
I used to have, and your outrageous laugh.
You move two glasses to one side and rest
the portrait in its frame against a jug.
Answer. Ask. Tinnitus butts in
beneath my breath or else his ghost
is whispering behind us. Reveries
belonging to last days of summer stir
inconsequentially. I read again
the slanting scribble in the bottom corner
and trace the spasm of the pen
that is his name. The sentiments
expressed seem pretty plainly yours.
The writing looks like mine, though firmer then.

Listening to Bees

There was a nest of bees up in the roof
when I was little and an aperture
in the eaves above my window and they came
and went through that. I hear the bees
in any room I'm in when I'm alone
if there's no TV in the corner croaking.
Still a child, but in another memory,
I'm being held in sunshine at that window
between the cool glass and a white lace curtain
my mother holds back with her head.
She wears it like a mantilla
and I am kicking, pushing arms and looking.
Please put me by the garden window now.
I've studied the electric busyness
of squirrels among branches of the trees.
They know what's suddenly enough.
They entertain and then they're gone
on hedges and a washing line. Today
I'd like to count the things that squirrels climb
and wear a curtain like a señorita
listening to bees with you, if you have time.
And if you've understood a word I've said.

The Old Stacks

It is not a fault in the iron, but a virtue, to be
so fond of getting rusted...

JOHN RUSKIN

Browsing in Afterlife, I won't reach up
for *Revelation* bound in the height of style
along with *Dénouement* or choose a weepy
in paperback that tells me the first day
death won't allow me to attain
starts out with dew on lawns and mist and early
scent of hawthorn hedges and that there's a tree
behind a damp slate roof that stands for home
which turns for autumn on the seaward side
beginning where the top leaves drip
with memory while those I loved who died
convene and are alive and sentimental.

No. I'll settle for a grave tome from the prime
of Britain's century, not *Origin*,
or *Adam Bede*, or Mill *On Liberty*,
but Ruskin with his spring and marble basin
where at the rim there is a saffron stain
like evidence of crime you can forget
until you're charged. My eyes will close
on clear water: iron and blood unseen
and nothing mirrored there, not sky, or time
dismantling my face, or even John
with art and artifice to reconcile
while through his mind a plague-wind blows.

The Better Place

Adam's dream will do here...

JOHN KEATS

Your day ain't over but old age has made
the twilight worrying. Towards the posh
end of the village are *cottages ornés*,
broad-eaved, with mullions, and chimneys
diagonally set. You'll find them fussy.
Too arty-farty for eternity.
Reflections have begun to fade from rosy
where the river now flows pearly neutral.
There's no bookshop. Though you'd have wished one once
you will not read. We'll speak in rhyme.
Thoughts are visible, resembling circling moths.
Another reason why this nook is suitable
is that although it's hilly Derbyshire
we're in a bowl and therefore there's a climb
to reach a view of genuine horizons
which you of course will have no need to see.
That house has character. The former smithy.
You might well settle there as aeons pass.
Meanwhile the radiant pub. The landlady
that Adam dreamed to serve your English breakfasts
and pull the empyreal ale that causes
such ardent listlessness. Fine suddenness.
And I shall be beside you by the fire
when in the evenings you think back to us.

(for S.J.K. and T.A.G.L.)

After Dark at Lindisfarne Castle

> The great commander of the Gormorants
> The Geese and Ganders of these Hallowed lands.

CAPTAIN RUGG

Here's the upper battery. Here is your ghost.
Thy presence seems composed, dear Captain Rugg,
of moistures of this summer night.
Thou didst not merely command cormorants
but culverins and demi-culverins,
sakers and falconets, master gunners,
a master's mate and then a score of sojers.
At this dainty fort you were a genial host
and strangers did abide. Your bottle nose
became a beacon in the dying light
of Britain's republic. I am not afraid.
Your hauntings hereabouts are just a jest,
thou hoaxer, Sir, thou hock of the hog,
thou gammon! Or are you waiting to be paid
by King or Parliament? You have no wants
your long-due wages could provide for now
methinks. I can make out, by looking through you,
lit windows of the borowgh toune all sett
with fishers very poore that is a markett
on ye Satterday, howbeit little used,
and then the tumbling Priory
that is the store-house of the garrison.
Perhaps we might talk poetry?
Like you, your couplets linger on.
But no, your nose swings further east
your finger to your lips and as you fade
I hear from off the Farnes the seals intone
the psalms that Cuthbert taught them as the sun
at dawn walks on the sea. I am alone.

Gantries

(i.m. Evangeline Paterson)

You believed in real heaven, no outrageous
life of spirit, endlessly delighting:
one poet fewer, one more butterfly
in some dim forest where a tiger smoulders.

We keep on borrowing each other's light,
and looking taller on each other's shoulders,
but you did neither and called out for less
confusion of the substance with the glitter.

You taught your poems to be homely,
as if their duty was to reassure,
and yet they scratch a question on the page
that angels from their gantries bend to answer.

The Magic Castle

Close the door. All she has managed to achieve
seems empty to her now. Throw in the towel.
Success is make-believe that fairytales
can easily transcend. So tell her one.
She's reached the ocean of self-doubt, its seas
acidic and tumultuous
and where their churning waters join
futures are born to serpents of the hour
enthroning bright new deities
whose joy is to propose annihilation
of well-tried methods and esprit de corps.
She's cleared her desk. The conference room
is shadowy. The girl she was
would stride the pine woods and bare northern hills
but she has booked retirement leave
among more tangled forest trees
where sun will warm deep pools of gloom
while she unbuttons her profession
to shed it and is glad to rest and weep
until the air cools and it's time to follow
charcoal burners or a witch or speaking owl
and find the magic castle where her life
has all these years been lived by someone else
like her, formidable but fast asleep.

The Unicorn

It has the body of a stallion
and paws the good earth with a razor hoof.
At first glance it's the lion's tail
he notices, and scarlet berries strewn
by female trees among a multitude
of hollies. Here in England light is snatched
by moiling clouds and won't return
while his life lasts. Take heed in looking back
lest you be taken, bold Sir Knight.
Don't rehabilitate old mania
or catch the itch that can't be scratched.
Alas, of hope there's none. His heart is true.
The glory of the realm must be restored
and loyal oaths be everywhere renewed.
He gleams. He's armoured head to foot in proof.
Thus cumbered he will not prevail.
He clamps his visor and unsheathes his sword
too late. The lethal forehead swerves,
transfixes him and hoists his weight.
He's dead before he drops. The holly leaves
become less sharp the higher up they grow.
The white neck of the terrible chimera
elongates to browse. It's tongue is quick.
It's tusk is slick with gore. His blood is blue.

Remission

She's digging with her hands for coloured glass
and losing contact with a finger end.
Meanwhile the light has turned less granular –
the bedroom re-emerging as it was
yesterday and all the days before. She's out
almost before she wakes. The path is wet.
Still in her night dress with a Barbour jacket
from off the hook beside the kitchen door
around her shoulders she surveys
the spreading weeds of her dog days
and glares up close at thistle flowers
like purple shaving brushes on which bees
are docking warily and with precision.

That movement in the distance must be me,
the morning shift arriving. It's too early
and too cold for crowing noises
she makes in greeting to resemble speech.
I round the the north side of the house to catch
her shivering where shrubs have overgrown
the front way in. I understand
how necessary it begins to seem
to juxtapose, while still there's time,
her past and future and explore
the busy dreams that link them. She insists
perversely that the work she pays me for
is simply friendship, while remission lasts.

LANDSCAPE WITH PSYCHE

Did heaven shape that heap of wonders
To be the dwelling of a snake?

PIERRE CORNEILLE

Her face is turned away. The sea is there.
The boat from which her sisters call
to urge that she must save herself by murder
is indistinct. So are their voices, shrill
in the quiet afternoon. A buck in line
with her long gaze has grazed for centuries
exactly where he stands. He will not raise
his antlered head to look yet holds in balance
her place and his within the composition.
Her mood is ours. The palace frowns
through carefully assembled trees
but shall admit her. She will listen hard
in shadows on a corner of the stairs
unreached by warm glow from the room he's in
where bottles clink and she can hear a murmur
of satisfied and god-like self-regard.
Sometimes Psyche loves the monster best, sometimes
her handsome man. Each seeks his opposite.
Lust thrives on curiosity. Meanwhile
where are the daylight gleam of prescious metal,
the promised pillars and the vaulted roof?
The wallpaper is scuffed. The building shrinks
to somewhere squalid that's not even his.
His motorbike and sidecar block
the ginnel slantwise and his friends squeeze past
rubbing against brick. The loudest
rests his hand against the wall and vomits
as they reach the street. Their quarrelling recedes
and Cupid settles down to drink alone
prodigiously, and for a decent swally
his teeth hinge backwards like a snake.
But this is what she fears not what she sees.
'Sovereign lady, all you see and fear is yours

together with the furies that beset you
with peril and with subterfuge.
Your servants, Ma'am. This is your narrative.
We are your train of ministering voices.
The painting we have found you in seems porous,
capacious, and so fluidly arranged
that it accommodates neglected altars,
envy and the winged bold boy. Your sisters
have left you hesitant. By all means stay
to eavesdrop and to tire your mind and suffer
and then put counsel into execution.
The light is dim. You have a torch
and you may find a sharp knife in the kitchen.'
One step at a time and anxious not to creak
she's coming down and will conceal
her contumacious beauty in a cupboard
underneath the stairs. The slant-parked Zephyr
is also beautiful. Beneath the stars
immortality is an horizon
forever in retreat. His recklessness
makes Cupid almost human. Orders come
from a pillion-creature shrieking shame and rage
provoked by her depleting charms
and ashes of old offerings. Right. Now left.
Turn back. Now right again. Only ourselves
could know her for a goddess in this fettle.
Or him a god despite his winged black leathers.
The air is clean but grabs the throat
like strangler's hands. Direction skids
and wheels turn idly like suspicions
that undermine the heart's felicity
with aftershock among the evening fields
where love sinks under settling dust.
He rights the bike and roars away
the sidecar empty, bashed awry. We dawdle
with prostrate Psyche and her lamentations.

'Dear Madam, you must look for work
assisting ants in warehouses of wheat
and barley, vetches, millet, beans and lentils
for nourishment of sharp-beaked doves of Venus,
or crossing torrents helped by speaking reeds
inspired by river gods and creeping
among the groves to gather golden wool
that clings to bushes and the trunks of trees
from fierce rams that will abide no shepherd.
Endure, and try your hand at anything.'
There's schwingmoor at the edge of Erebus,
a place to linger and to weave
insectivorous and poisonous garlands.
And there's a gate into a field
where mud sucks boots and then a perilous
approach by quivering moss a metre thick
above black depths to where the ferry lands
to take her to beseech of Proserpine
a box of beauty brighter than her own.
She must not open it and yet she does.
A fetid stink hangs in the air. She squelches
through dripping boskage among clawing briars.
She will need cash, for there is greed
even among the dead, and sandwiches
to share with Cerberus. Despite her hurry
she is admiring stalk-stiff bulrushes
whose heads split open every Spring
and fill the air with seeds. A sign:
No Hoping Is Allowed Beyond This Point.
The picture-space we look into contains
all this within a still reality
that rests on artifice. The woods
cohere in huddled colloquy
beneath a listening sky. Cupid's abode
presents a high pillastered front
pierced by lightless windows. The entablature

has obelisks above a balustrade.
Older rounded towers recede. It looms.
It is the setting for what we imagine
is due to Psyche. Whatever happens
will not disturb Claude's contemplative buck
grazing in the seventeenth-century rooms.
He digests myth. He ruminates.
Like him, we're thoughtful and half-close our eyes
to minimise reflected light.
'My lady, you are the bearer of a gift
of beauty from the Queen of Shades herself,
shall you not have the right to dab a smidjin
on your already lovely cheeks and thus
acquire advantage in your husband's eyes?'
She lifts the lid but there is nothing there
except a Stygian fart that drifts
across the pavement out into the traffic.
She slumps on tarmac and inhales
erasure of her senses. This is death
if Cupid will not come on dewy wings
with ringlets on his neck and snowy brow
to gather up her sleep and close the box.
And how would Soul then couple with Desire?
Her sisters rent a place where every night
consists of living for the day.
We take a taxi through an inner-city
to find their clothes-strewn flat-share and a glass
or three of hooch. News of her dire misfortune
delights them privily for now
they scheme that Cupid will choose one of them.
Each by herself next groggy morning heads
homeward, though not to Mum and Dad, bereft
of Psyche in their close-shut house,
but to an eyrie near the peak
of Kawasaki, crying out to Zephyr
to bear them in their glad-rags to his lord.

They are swept up bodily but not sustained
above the precipice to which their spite
and envy took them to be dashed to pieces.
The seasons crimson all things with their roses.
No one winds the clocks on Mount Olympus.
Cupid and Psyche's special day
has no beginning and no end. The party
swings forever. The gods are there.
They've trashed the place and revellers
spill into the street. The police
are on their way eternally.
Floorboards are ripped up. Walls are kicked and scratched.
The music is unbearable.
Carvings and paintings representing beasts
of the chase and rustic scenes adapted
to please the eye are shamefully defaced.
The state apartments have been wrecked.
Jewellery and rare productions
of craftsmanship and nature all together
with sumptuous hangings have gone walkabout.
A knife is missing from a kitchen drawer.
Neighbours in Arcadia have been assured
that grief like this gets zero-tolerance.
But round here it's still tough mythology.
'Madam, let's slip away from such shenanigans
to Cupid's halls, where you shall reign
though mortal as immortal queen.
Your manly god will not at all resemble
a loathsome serpent but a comely youth
who's on the wagon now. The bike is sold.
There is no call for murder and his mother
condescends to visit. We, your faithful train
of voices, croak. As we grow old
enjoyments and refinements mellow us.'
In a chamber with a view beyond the sea
through painted trees into a hushed museum,

ages away yet near, where connoisseurs
pause among undisputed masterworks
savouring the smell of polish,
our afternoon is witnessing
the birth of Pleasure. She is our child too.
All is resolved. The buck lifts up his head
and Venus remounts her throne. Her altars glow.
Psyche warms to nectar and ambrosia
but will not claim comparison
with She, fountain of elements.
That's all that we remember. Paparazzi
flash pictures of her as a butterfly.
The heavenly assembly drinks a toast
to perpetuity. We echo it.
While those below, who could not help but kiss
their fingertips at sight of her,
forget and are themselves in time forgotten,
the gods refresh their taste for human beauty.

The Turtle Holiday

There is no better place to contemplate
his distant bedsit with its rack
of shabby attitudes he posed in once
than by this over-photographed lagoon
where creatures of prodigious weight
wallow. He has not found the atmosphere
helpful in making friends or sense.
Even his pockets have remained unpicked.
He's glad it's his last evening. Temperature
is poised. There is no climate and no barrier
between his mind and moonlit night,
the clutch of warm sand and the click
of knocked shells broadcasting under water
the signal he is trying not to hear.

Proxy

Stay here and be myself but sick and old,
the wreck of me, my Brother Ass
spavined and irresolute. I've set you down
in a courtyard with wisteria
and darkening lemon leaves and water play.
White houses and a church comprise the town
with shallow roofs and storks' nests. We have seen,
as we approached, the sweep of bay
towards the cliff and have discussed
distant palid mainland and the golden
hem of the horizon and the ocean
acting blue for us. My friend, this is the crust
on the pie of suffering. Tuck in.
I wish you well. Goodbye. I'm young again.

Next Time

Church-smell holds my breath. There is a flutter
high in the roof as if the Holy Ghost
embodied by a bird has lost Her way
between a moment and its memory.
A spider crossing in an eightsome skelter
blood-glow of stained glass did so already.
My time is dwindling but I can't adjust
to squeeze myself into a smaller future
while *That was now* and *This is then* are twisting
recall and attention out of kilter.
The fluttering has reached my head. The spider
has found its way again to unlit dust.
Cool stillness is complete, a silence bruised
and waiting till I come back yesterday.

The Winpole Boy

All the symptoms pointed to bhurine...
ERNEST BRAMAH

His first glance will take in the lofty ceiling,
good china, and a damask portière.
Next he may notice recesses.
Cross-lights from glass doored cabinets
reflecting fading dusk from windows set
in panelling catch filmy dust. Take care!
A table tilts and tumbles loudly spilling
notebooks and chemicals beside the fire
in spite of which he's shivering.
Under a bhurine bottle – smashed to bits
and deadly – lies the reason for his visit:
the recipe that could ensure we'll find
all we've ever lost the very minute
that it's no longer missed or called to mind.

After Pevsner

To appreciate the house it must be seen
in the radiance emitted by its own
baroque bravura and immensity.
Although the hills are softened by plantation
the contrast with surrounding barrenness
shocks each time it shows itself so that our eyes
are locked until they are released
to strain again to watch it fade from view.
As someone said, in fact a novelist:
'It is as if I'm shown a masterpiece
secreted in a grotto, or a statue
of a goddess in her splendour in a barn.'
No one can get there easily or soon.
The heights of its estates command the passes.

The Nuisances

We sneak on velvet feet and speak or squeak
as if our needs were paws exploring fridges
or bees in foxgloves. She's the blur
in which the dry leaves rattle in light gusts
of revelation and the elder bushes
exhale a stale milk smell. Wise butterflies
perch on her forehead. Stingless midges
fall prey to the tall bird with the long glass beak
she knows from visits to its many nests.
It will at times regurgitate to feed her.
We pester her as she weaves necklaces
from flowers she finds with children's faces
and beg to be her guests or ghosts.
Sometimes she bites our tongues to punish us.

Pastoral

(for Alistair Elliot)

Wherever I can find a meadow, ghosts
of mowers move in line like handwriting
across grass readied for the scythe by dew.
I'm shadowing their shadows, on their heels
and in their balance and their rhythm breathing
to stride into the cut and tug a string
tight to stop a frightened vole from running
up a trouser leg. There's laughter here and song
exactly at the moment of its loss.
And I shall loiter among sheaves
to drink the peace they leave, the purple glow
when they go home down lanes and into graves.
I'm aftermath, foggage and bullimong,
an upstart in the poetry of fields.

The Ornithologist

New rain has left the footpaths even wetter
but clouds are clearing. There'll be sun
to finish off the day. He is offended –
this much at least we understand –
at our discourtesy and so he searches
the woods with his binoculars, the better
to brood and to compare what has been said
with previous lapses in respect. His ears
are burning. He's a laughingstock.
We'll have to leave him to it in the end.
Saying sorry smacks of condescension
and all our this-will-buck-you-up ideas
are like weak whistles from a flock
of little long-tailed birds through silver birches.

Resting Rats

Oaks grown beyond maturity will totter
both in my head and out there on the hill.
They are consolidated memory
in the entorhinal cortex, rocked by gales
of new impressions from the hippocampus
and yet preserved and stabilised
for swift recall by sleep. One great one fell
and half my life ago its root plate tore
a chunk of slope away. Today
such processes are better understood
thanks to Dr Freyja Ólafsdóttir
and research done on resting rats. The tree
lies grey and textured like a brain, a blurry
oak-wreck that's no longer wood or timber.

Virgil

Bright sunshine will distort what it reveals.
Politicians like the light. We're strung along.
This afternoon I rubbed my thumb
around the chipped rim of a coffee cup
and thought what could be worse. A shining gulf
might be decreed, dividing day from night.
Penumbra though, which public glare conceals,
will long outlast deceit and pelf.
At work there is the genius by whom
gloaming was first written down. The shepherd youth
Nostalgia, arm in arm with sister Hiraeth,
is with him and still prompts him into song
in groves where milk-white peacocks droop
their ghostly tails and squawk the truth.

French Windows

The folly tower you noticed from the train
and thought of for the rest of one short journey
when you were young is where I choose to linger.
On all your birthdays I unfurl a banner
above the decorative battlements.
I do not age. I don't forget.
Once there were people here. They went away
through tall French windows borrowed from the set
of some old-fashioned comedy
and left behind a well-found elegance.
The place is nowhere that a connoisseur
would classify as an essential structure
but stands its ground with dignity.
It would have suited you. Where have you been?

The Philosopher

I glimpsed a pale observer. I explored
upstairs to find his room, and here it is.
The key is stiff. I shake my head
away from cobwebs. There's a second door
blocked off by bookcases. An old fur coat
across an armchair has begun to shed.
A plaster bust of a philosopher
on the dusty window ledge is set in place
as if to watch the garden where I stood,
the golf course and the dunes, and then the sea.
The heavy air is cooling as the day
wears on. The thought-struck face at this late hour
begins reflecting in the darkening glass
and all there is to ponder on is me.

Barefooted

In a bid to dodge yet one more platitude,
she asks him who he really is
or if he cannot tell her then to fake
an interesting past. He does admit
that on the long drive down he passed a lake
which had the full moon shining brightly on it
and felt that he could walk across
barefooted. It is possible
she says that one might do that and return
to shore but subsequently drown
in disappointment and conclude
that beauty is deceit and always was.
He fails to prepossess. He's dull.
But she is greedy and takes off his shoes.

The Trouser Button

The chair on which he sits or rather kneels
is ergonomically designed.
His desk and window both look out
not onto distances but at the top
of his prized magnolia tree. Leaves shiver
to manifest the movement of a breeze
which he now also hears and feels.
The window shrugs. He thinks. He makes a note.
Objects may be inanimate yet quiver.
A trouser button in a puddle tries
to sing. Though insignificant
and even pitiful it has a soul
as we do. And through art, he writes, our goal
is to commune with it. The wind has dropped.

Sanquar

The good man pauses as if in a frame
between the gatepiers of the cemetery –
corniced, and each topped with a pyramid –
and looks apologetically
regretful that I've spotted him.
He comes to make sure that the dead
sleep tight beneath the stone of Rachel Hair,
together with her child. Both died
to save his life once in a brawl
with Cromwell's Ironsides. It's in the form
of two adjoining coffins, big and small.
As if he were to blame for history,
the good man haunts the town each night in shame
because he is not buried with them there.

LADDEREDGE AND COTISLEA

We thought we were living now,
but we were living then.

ANNE STEVENSON

Towards the farm at which I am permitted
inside the barn and then to climb the hay bales
is an old man with a scythe says Youngster
unwrapping as I skip to greet him sacking
from the blade. He slides the stone along
long time. I think I see my mother's hand
withdrawn from drawing curtains at a window
slip back into that room with the aroma
of nearly damp encyclopaedias.
Mind can touch mind. I feel my tongue
begin to press the past. The box
that sits on the table called Occasional
her fingers rest upon has mirrored drawers
whose memories are asking me to speak.
The chimney whispers to the clean cold hearth.

The brave boys that have gone away
will march back home one sunny day.

You can't get what you need for love nor money.
I do not understand how that it is
the opposite direction for the lane
will join the road towards a future farther
than Buxton is or Macclesfield and people
After the War Before the War
are selling what they do to live. It's called
the World of Work. It's in a dream
I hear them talk. I'm half awake.
What can you do? There aren't the men.
There is a doll to be undressed
and school books of my uncles who are dead
but aren't dead now of course but are Called Up
like Daddy who I don't know yet.

It seems you have an interest in silence
and oily dust where nothing is disturbed
in which case you will want to hear
about an Austin Seven up on blocks
behind its blistered garage doors
and petrol rations. There's a fox
all night in Mollock's Wood. I think he tries
to sing to me. I am asleep.

And with the big girls in the gorse
who tell things and play Truth Or Dare or worse.

Caterpillar Tractor is the best thing.
Milk Cart though comes every morning
with that horse has a name that I can say
but I don't know it now. The dippers clatter
with different voices and are big and little
to lift milk from the churn. Someone is laughing.
The same hand from the curtains holds the jug.
I paint an outhouse door with Dolly Blue
which makes it wet not blue. Another fox
I think sings like the one I know at night
up on the roof the wind turns. Later a pond
has a spit where I will dig a grave
among the tree roots where I know
it is the best place for a Viking cat.
As well in future I will have my bus fare
to where the vet lives and back with her dead.
That place will also be where Harvey
shows us his Circumcision. Up the lane
the cows come which have heavy tails.
I stalk them in my wellingtons.

Another laugh. Jam Rags on the line. A shout.
Toys in a van. Demobbed. The air is soot.

The ceiling light hangs like a chandelier
with fitments where gas mantles were
and has a middle that's a crown.
It has to go and crashes. I will try
to wear it in a cloud of dust.
Daddy is hammering. Outside air is clean.
At night I shall not hear the fox.
But in the day is Blow Lamp. Paint comes off.
Even Lincrusta. The house is old
and has a cellar but will be like new.
The curtains are not wide enough.
Hands will bring poppers that will keep them shut
and rise to stitch against the sun.
The house is in a marl field. That means clay.
And where the pond is it is like a lake.
The Viking sea. I have a Siren Suit
and talk to grown-up children at the gate
when street lights being lit. I think I've come
a long way off and they don't like my name.

It's nearly Christmas what it is. I wake
in time for Daddy's Home Now motorbike.

The bully has a needle with a hilt
like a sword. It is a hat pin.
He is the torturer outside the outside
lavatory. He shall stay where air is soot.
I'll make a notice for a Zoo and tie it
big to the garden gate. No one will come.
There's just the goldfish and the toad
that's always in the coal-shed but today
is not. I do not know what's true when that is
but you will know by now. We're on a Walk.
Mummy that's the hands and Daddy
and pushchair Margaret. I find butter
in fresh packets hid behind a tree beside

the path where no one lives. It is Black Market
so we will take it home and not
Waste Time Worrying. Another day
we hear a voice that shouts *A Murrain On Ye*
at us from a bleak barn with an echo.

Christmas occurs and Santa Claus
and tears and frightening said and slamming doors.

There is a worse dream or maybe a part
that happens on its own and seems
more anxious. There are lavatories again
but this time made by sculptors out of junk
like driftwood with some paint adhering, toys
and car parts and with various containers.
Some are stuck up in the air and shaky
and some are squelchy underground.
The creatures that are queueing see right in.
They don't know me. Though some are nice
most are indifferent and grunt
or if they seem like women they will sigh.
I should have something that I do to sell
but all I've got is words they grab
and look at upside down. It is the World
of Work. They cannot read but like to feel
the paper. Martin lives in a Council House.
His Dad has a shed with tools. One day he lets
us have a log and hammers and a bag
of panel pins. We knock them in
and trying not to bend them till the log
is heavy Heaven with a thousand stars.

You only need to blink to think
about me and the years between us shrink.

The Tip is where we go along the track
out into fields by Whittle's shop.
You smell it burning and not breathing parts
are sticky hot. That's where we find what treasure
is to play with. There are gas masks and helmets
and sometimes German ones and bayonets
and bicycles to put together bits.
There's a story that's got me in it before
all that which Mummy tells she laughs about.
Perhaps you'll laugh as well for listening.
The Combine Harvester has stopped
and waits and tucks its shadow in. It's time
for sandwiches and lemonade
but there are men with guns around the island
that is still standing crop. I hear the rustle
of the rabbits very frightened and the hares
as well there with me and the shotgun barrels
click into place. What happens is
that my red hat and me are glimpsed
in one small movement of the corn.
The guns are lowered and the air is heavy
and by my movement and because that moment
I shall live as long as you exactly.
Mummy what are you thinking of
or chatting to a Land Girl without thought?
There is another Walk and when it's frosty
so Magic Lane is pink because the sky
and there are clouds shaped like a T
because it's Time for Tea which Daddy says.
I race him home. He lets me win.

Who has a mo-mo off the Tip?
Whose little mo-mo says Pip Pip?

Up the road I must not where are different
children is a pumping station
abandoned with a bashed-in door
with old machinery and rust
and knee-deep water trouble happens with.
The different children Mummy says are Rough.
This summer there is hidden grass
between the clumps of gorse up at the top
of Back Field where the big girls are
that show their knickers. It's tea-time again
but late and Daddy in the distance looking.
Uncle George is not my uncle
but Mr Gibson who makes cider
drip through straw that smell I like.
One day I shall say odoriferous
and sesquipedalian for you too.
He saws a Walking Stick be short for me.
Now when the sun keeps still I go
down in the big weeds living in his garden
to where it's warming at a wall where once
upon a time he tied an Animal.
It has an iron ring that hangs
to put my nose in that's still low enough
for me wherever it has gone to now.

Pig in the book has nose that has a ring
so ring has nose will be a funny thing.

But in another dream my head slides through
and then I see it. I am on my own
more frightened now than ever I remember
and footsteps on the landing in the night
until I pay attention. What I say
even in the sun that's in the garden
or in the wood where foxes sing
goes to a dark mask in a circular

hat shape that's huge and is an ear as well
and like the inside of a black umbrella.
But it will also go to you–that's-me –
an old man in an armchair looking back.
The other fox does not turn in the wind
above my bed but on a different roof
on Woodside Lane one day he winks
when Mummy *Look At Fox* and lifts me up.
The work that is the world is time.

Daddy will crank my bed into a car.
I drive to sleep. He did not like the War.

Down the road there is a Bottling Machine
and Sour that is the bad smell. Mr Clayton
brings milk with a Milk Float now and has no horse
but Ferrets that want all the time to eat
my fingers. I'm putting off the worst thing.
This summer too is time for Dens
in Coppice Wood and Mollock's Wood to hide
and hunt and find the others first.
I have forgotten home is where-am-I
once more when Daddy worried so of course
it's not the first occasion or the last
and it is not the worst thing which is what
it is that only happens once for ever.
In due course we shall come to that.
Biffs to the head will cause imagination.
But Mummy says I worry him too much
about me that I'll worry him to death.

I've watched my father reach for breath and die.
I'm reading Biggles. Boys don't cry.

I see the place he used to hang
his leather Crash Hat and his Goggles
are hidden somewhere what I think
and Gauntlets gone were on the kitchen chair.
But may I still go out to play?
September's coming and with engines chewing
fog and steam and smoke and fire and hauling
vacant carriages with sepia photographs
and luggage racks like fishing nets and me
along the soon closed Churnet Valley Line
to stop at Rudyard Lake, Cliffe Park and Rushton,
Bosley Halt, North Rode and Macclesfield.
And School. But that is always afterwards.
There's also in this summer time for jousting
on bikes with six foot garden canes
from Firth's the shop for everything.
The aim is not to stick an eye
and that could happen but to get the lance
between the spokes and throw him off.
We all have proper shields not dustbin lids
and helmets from the Tip to beat each other
with heavy sticks. It is the Middle Ages
and violent and innocent.
But there is Keith from Sunday School
too old for us who comes to show us fireworks
kept back from Bonfire Night and mice
and frogs blown up and what he does
to insects that have wings and legs.
He has a girlfriend too and tells us what
she does that's what he makes her do.
On a lawn by Woodside Lane a mower leaves
the smell that is the panic of the grass.

I think you think that what I say is Now
which means that I am nearly you.

I'm down among the dreams again and dreaming
about the big black hat that is the ear
of sleep and voices that I love the most
go silent there for ever and inside it –
Greased Lightning gone as quick as that –
and also of the mirror box
that falls from the table called Occasional
and shatters me awake. Footsteps come and hands
at night in August half-light by the marl field.
It doesn't really break. My face looks back
at me-that's-you from every drawer
but something is that sort happening she says
and pulls beside herself and me to Daddy.
We are too proud to have The Telephone
and can't afford it anyway
so she has gone to rouse them at the Dairy
but I can watch him and I always shall
where it is almost dawn and hear him breathe
like slow strokes of the stone along
long time and loud then sudden louder stop.
The scythe is sharp and I think Good.

I sold the world a life for time to do
this work for nothing, finding words for True.

The Gypsy Fiddle

The garden wall is higher than two men
but he is free to roam the lawn
as if it were a world. He greets the day
with a shrill aubade and spreads his palms to swear
the oath that binds him never to disclose
the secrets of his race or teach the cant
to dommerars or patricoes,
abrams, Irish toyles or clapperdogeons
and always to share out in fellowship
what he can steal from libkins or the ruffmans
while cleaving stiffly to a doxy wap.
He'll bring her duds, tibs of the buttery,
margery praters, grunting cheats,
as winnings for her weppings. As if their rags
were ropes to tie them they will be as one
in all the thievings he imagines.
His lamentations are heartfelt and subtle
and he can grip a tune. Although he eats
more like a beast than human creature
and has no ready ribbin he'll not want
for peckage. The light fades. He has earned a nap.
Beside the rockery a deck chair sags
where he is resting like a gypsy fiddle
from which the bow has been withdrawn.

The Columns

One autumn morning on her way to school
to be instructed and admonished
by a donkey wearing spectacles,
she left behind her gang of playful shadows
because the world seemed brightly real and better
and chose a longer unfamiliar route,
completely uncurricular –
although she was in fact the donkey's daughter –
which led her to a clearing in a wood
where there were columns by a pool
which steeped them upside down and still. She saw
that some were chiselled smooth and some were fluted
and some with ornate capitals were tall,
others abruptly short. Some were embellished
with signs she could not read and some had fallen.

The world seemed darkly abstract then and worse,
and there, expecting her to come,
was a question older than she'd ever be.
She took it with her to the classroom lit
by lofty windows onto sky,
but no one noticed in the chalky air
among shrill voices of the teachable.
The donkey, though ridiculous,
was erudite, but she could not remember
from that day on a single thing it taught,
or exercise her mind at all unless
to think how best to get the question home,
unacknowledged and as if forgotten,
to where the columns are, unreachable
as their reflections in unrippled water.

The Vapour Trail

On the west side of the room there is a set
of three large windows. It will be
perhaps her favourite spot. It's getting dark
but she remains preoccupied
by what she felt at sunset when she looked
above the looming shrubbery
to see a vapour trail light up, blood-red,
and cut the sky. She drops her coat
across a packing-case and flicks
the light switch as she wonders where to start.
It's best, she has been told – the first
time sweeping any house – that it's done *inward*,
so good luck isn't lost like dust.
But memories, she thinks, should be swept *out*
with all their hurt. Then check each door is locked.

An Exhibition Catalogue

He felt both crushed and broke in war-time London's
black-outs and shortages and learned the art
of circulating as a perfect guest.
He chose to paint – I quote – *the naked figure*
in strange conjunctures, merging ground and body,
genetics and geology,
in sensual rage mocked by a universe
indifferent to mortal pain or comfort...

His inspiration were the labourers
at work in gardens of the country houses
where owners of the landscape were his patrons
and underwrote the hurricane of effort
which blew itself out in these late canvasses
depicting hybrids, vegetal and human –
always unquestionably male –
contorting among trunks of trees...

Students seem to like the stuff, and connoisseurs
of what they call The New Apocalypse.
But speaking for myself, I have to say
it always prompts a quasi-smile
with no relationship at all to pleasure,
that sharp contraction of a frown
into a mirthless and dismissive gesture
which grips a critic's face when patience snaps.

Death and the Spinster

The problem is, now I'm alone and old,
that mirrors also start to age and tarnish.
Tonight let's look in one of them together
and ponder our proximity.
Press up tight behind my shoulder.
I will do my best to focus
on each of us in turn until I'm sure
we've got a clear joint-portrait in reverse.
Don't think I'm fostering a tenderness
for the grotesque. I dread the day
when all reflections lose themselves for ever
among the flaws and whorls of antique glass.
Even now, fine crazing and pale mustard-brown
discolourations spread out to obscure
the features I'm most eager to behold –
my blushing cheeks, your smile of bone,
the fondness that is evident between us –
and I forget how beautiful we are.

The Cormorant

Then up he flew, and on the Tree of Life,
The middle Tree and highest that there grew,
Sat like a Cormorant...

JOHN MILTON

You only slipped up once but here I am
inside the arched door in your garden wall
hell-bent on mischief in thin milky air
my hand behind me on the heavy latch.
I feel its weight and smell what you no doubt
would think of as the gratitude
of warm damp earth. The storm has passed.
A wind-swerve delicately propped a ladder
against the glass of the conservatory
at a flamboyant angle. Plants in pots
including heavy ones have been upset
and are unbroken, but the mind
we used to be content to share
fractured at the point at which nostalgia
gusted into fury. Tics of imbalance
mimic action as I hold my pose and smile.
I own your past and I have planned your future
without a thought for innocence or gardens.
All you achieved will vanish under steel
and glass and concrete where the light retreats
from devilishly self-projecting shadows
and I will perch myself grown huge
above what little good you ever managed
while cannibals and victims eagerly
invoke the angels of the internet
to swap addresses and contrive to meet.

Seasons

We can be certain that this world is dumb.
Yet I am shown a photograph
of landscape clothed in tints of autumn rust
with a tree in it my interlocutress
maintains she never finds again, no matter
how many times she goes back there to look.
She says it spoke when she stood under it
and she feels obligated to respond.
Winter is gathering. A blast of sleet
melts on her balcony and drips
from metal furniture. The damp air nips.
Insentient and inarticulate,
the objects that surround us don't require
an answer, ever, and to offer one
seems to my mind at the very least perverse.
My friend will not agree. I feel her laugh
first as a cool draught, then a gust
of warmer and more spring-like air, a flutter
against my neck and throat that climbs
towards my ear and turns into a whisper
of wind through leaves elsewhere where it's still summer.

News of a Death

Her mind's eye wakes but ordinary sight
is working too. She is aware
of noticing the neatness of her quarters
and glancing at haphazard things –
a book left open face-down on her bed,
the hat she wore this morning for her stroll
on deck hung on the shoulder of a chair.
And on her dressing table there's a sheet
of the ship's own notepaper, a hair brush
and a pen. A deepening vibration
of distant engines through the hull could mean
a change of course or more resistant sea.
He's here. He lifts a hand as if to say
that everything has been already said.
He disappears, and right away
she hears a voice that holds no doubt or fear
confirm within herself the temperament
to face unflappably what cannot be.
By dawn the weather's worsening. She sees
her porthole darken as an albatross
with fiery sunlight on its wings
glides past as in a ritual
and turns to look at her in both her eyes.

My Mother at Erbistock

The river is and carries off the rain
that came with summer thunder in the heart
of Wales to England and the sands of Dee.
A butterfly, where beech roots sieve the flow
falls upwards through the rungs of air.
You would have noticed it and told its name.
White noise incessant on the weir
drowns children's laughter happy in the day
before their futures start. To call us home,
to call us home with every memory
and all that love you had for time
when family coheres is what you do.
Down where the bank is shallower
swallows slip anchor in reflected blue.
I'm still your child that was. Hold tight my arm.
We'll wade together now and turn the sky
once more to ripples of the brown flood water.

A Piano in Hobart

(for Michael and François)

If tuning turns out to be difficult
the fault most often lies in weaknesses
and instabilities. Lest we forget,
now we begin to walk and talk, the thin
memorial flame becomes more visible
as sunlit dazzle yields to spats of rain.
The grass has recently been mown.
Sometimes the soundboard's curvature
together with the angle of a string
become exaggerated and display
crucial points most under pressure
from struggles with the tension of the steel
towards best pitch. The estuary
is broadening beyond the cenotaph
in order to become the sea.
Each string bears eighty kilograms of stress.
That's twenty tonnes. The metal frame
is made to stiffen the harmonic structure
but not constrict the breath of sound.
Mount Wellington pulls down the cloud. Up there
Spring weather has not yet arrived.
Two world wars are commemorated here
together with Korea and Malaya,
Indonesia and Vietnam
and lives mislaid away from home.
The layered wood and metal of the wrestplank
is also subject to intense
and searing pressure. Birdsong for a moment
is drawing out a wine cork squeakily
unlike the wood grain of the resonator
which is compressed so pulsing qualities,
in step with melody and harmony

and their affinities, are amplified
before transmission to the ear. This morning
we're at the birthplace of Van Diemen's Land.
Brass studs set in the pavement mark the route
the causeway took like an umbilicus.
Mother ships moored off the isthmus nourished
trade and settlement. Here is the School of Art.
In time a wrestplank can succumb to bending
and tip forward. Its pin housings,
affected by repeated chords,
becoming oval in severest cases.
The pins themselves may fail, worn out and rusted.
And here's the Institute of Engineering
in Tudor style but with a roof
of corrugated iron and a pole
to fly a flag which strains the rope. Rotations
repeated frequently make screw threads dull.
It's pleasanter to listen to ourselves
in cities we may never see again
although we hope. This ambling chat
revives young aspirations. Fully loaded,
strings must hold at their required tension
without detachment of the soundboard ribs.
The Drunken Admiral is closed
to thirsty brawlers, disembarked
two hundred years ago. Piano wire,
rail tracks and corrugated came
ashore from Hunter Island on the strength
of sailors and convicted men. Remember
that all adjustment has an influence,
even when meticulous and limited
to one part only, on the entire thing.
The Quarantine Shed stood where a building site
promises residential luxury
but there or anywhere disintegration
will come at last to a pianoforte

or any many-layered construction
be it an instrument of art and pleasure,
of comprehension, or of memory,
and also make an end of who we are
dans cette vie. Merci, François. Thank you, Michael.
Fountain water breezes sideways
to kiss our faces as we turn toward
Salamanca one last time. Old tuners dread
the snap of tarnished strings grown stiff with age,
and old geographers intuited
the Southern continents because they knew
without them that the world would topple over
becoming music we will never hear.

NOTES

The Comfort Service (18): In 1926 the photographer Don Gillum took publicity shots of a very uneasy Greta Garbo posing with MGM's mascot, Leo the Lion. The lion belonged to Randall Jarrell's aunt.

La Morale de Joujou (21): In his essay *'La Morale de joujou'*, written in 1853, Baudelaire explains that children want to see the soul of a toy. They will shake it, hurl it at the ground, and often break it in their bafflement and rage at its refusal to awaken into life.

A Helpmeet for Protestant Mystics (22): In 'The Protestant Mystics', W.H. Auden asserts that there are four sorts of mystical vision: that of God, that of Agape, that of Eros, and that of Dame Kind. The essay doesn't mention a helpmeet.

The Old Stacks (28): Charles Darwin's *On the Origin of Species*, George Eliot's *Adam Bede*, John Stuart Mill's *On Liberty*, and John Ruskin's *The Two Paths*, which includes 'The Work of Iron', were published in 1859. In later life Ruskin became convinced that a 'plague-wind' was blowing over Britain.

The Better Place (29): In a letter to Benjamin Bailey, written in November 1817, Keats tells his friend that 'we shall enjoy ourselves here after (sic) by having what we called happiness on Earth repeated in a finer tone... Adam's dream will do here...'. Elsewhere he recommends 'ardent listlessness' and 'fine suddenness' as good states of mind for poetry. Adam's dream is described in Book VIII of *Paradise Lost*.

After Dark at Lindisfarne Castle (30): The National Trust Guide Book to Lindisfarne Castle provided the information about Captain Rugg.

Remission (34): I am grateful to Dr Paul Evans, writing in the *Country Diary* column of the *Guardian*, for his description of thistles.

Landscape with Psyche (35): Paul Valéry also used the quotation from *Psyché*, by Pierre Corneille, as the epigraph of *La Jeune Parque*, translated here by Alistair Elliot. The painting in my poem is *Landscape with Psyche outside the Palace of Cupid*, 1664, by Claude Lorraine, in the National Gallery, London. Here and there I have borrowed phrases from the story of Cupid and Psyche, from *The Golden Ass* by Apuleius, as retold by Thomas Bulfinch and Walter Pater in 1855 and 1885.

The Winpole Boy (45): In 'Who Killed Charlie Winpole?', Ernest Bramah notes that bhurine does not occur naturally except as a constituent of Amanita Bhuroides, or the Black Cap, also known as the Devil's Scent Bottle. One fifth of a grain would be fatal to an adult. I have not found this toadstool mentioned elsewhere.

After Pevsner (46): The poem borrows from and alters a description of Drumlanrig Castle. The novelist is Daniel Defoe, but this is not exactly what he said.

Resting Rats (50): In April 2016 an article in *Nature Neuroscience* reported on research carried out on resting rats by Dr Freyja Ólafsdóttir, of University College London, into processes by which the brain stores memories, which it is thought may lead to improvements in the treatment of Alzheimer's disease.

Virgil (51): This poem was written in June 2016, after a referendum about Britain's membership of the European Union. According to Erwin Panofsky and others, Virgil invented evening. Oscar Wilde mentions 'milk-white peacocks', quoting from Tennyson's poem 'Now Sleeps the Crimson Petal', in his essay 'The Decay of Lying', 1891, in which he similarly claims that poets gave us the language of twilight.

The Trouser Button (55): In *Man and his Symbols*, edited by C.G. Jung, Aniela Jaffé quotes Wassily Kandinski: 'Everything that is dead quivers. Not only the things of poetry, stars, moon, wood, flowers, but even a white trouser button glistening out of a puddle in the street... Everything has a secret soul, which is silent more often than it speaks.'

Ladderedge and Cotislea (57): The poem revisits memories from between my war-time early childhood and my father's death in 1953. I was born at Ladderedge, near Leek, in Staffordshire. Cotislea is the name of a house my family lived in later, in Poynton, in Cheshire.

The Gypsy Fiddle (67): I am indebted to *A Classical Dictionary of the Vulgar Tongue* by Francis Grose, originally published in 1785.

The Cormorant (72): The epigraph is from Book IV of *Paradise Lost*, lines 194–196.

My Mother at Erbistock (75): There is an echo here of Charles Kingsley's poem 'The Sands of Dee'. Erbistock is on that river.